For Ben, Martha, Incas, George, Toughie, Turgi, Benjamin, Celia...
and all of the late, great and nameless others.

—D.K.

With love to my family and friends near and far,
and with gratitude to the first and best artist, Mother Nature.

—A.v.D.

Text copyright © Deborah Kerbel 2022
Illustrations copyright © Aimée van Drimmelen 2022

Published in Canada and the United States in 2022 by Orca Book Publishers.
orcabook.com

Library and Archives Canada Cataloguing in Publication
Title: The late, great endlings : stories of the last survivors / Deborah Kerbel ; illustrated by Aimée van Drimmelen.
Names: Kerbel, Deborah, author. | Van Drimmelen, Aimée, illustrator.
Identifiers: Canadiana 2021034511X | ISBN 9781459827660 (hardcover) | ISBN 9781459827677 (PDF) | ISBN 9781459827684 (EPUB)
Subjects: LCSH: Endangered species—Juvenile literature. | LCSH: Extinction (Biology)—Juvenile literature.
Classification: LCC QL83 .K47 2022 | DDC J591.68—dc23

Library of Congress Control Number: 2021948781

Summary: This STEM-based illustrated nonfiction picture book introduces readers to
several well-known animal and insect endlings, the last known survivors of a species, while discussing
the mass-extinction crisis facing our planet and what kids can do to make a difference.

Orca Book Publishers is committed to reducing the consumption of nonrenewable resources in the production of our books.
We make every effort to use materials that support a sustainable future.

Orca Book Publishers gratefully acknowledges the support for its publishing programs provided by
the following agencies: the Government of Canada, the Canada Council for the Arts and
the Province of British Columbia through the BC Arts Council and the Book Publishing Tax Credit.

Artwork created with watercolor and ink, including natural inks made by the artist.

Cover and interior artwork by Aimée van Drimmelen
Edited by Liz Kemp
Design by Rachel Page

Printed and bound in South Korea.

25 24 23 22 • 1 2 3 4

The Late, Gr Endling

Stories of th Last Survivor

Deborah Kerbel

Illustrated by
Aimée van Drimmelen

ORCA BOOK PUBLISHERS

You know about the dodo bird,
great auk and dinosaur—
lost creatures that once shared our world
so many years before.

But something that you may not know:
in each and every case
of a disappearing species,
extinction had a face.

Behold the late, great endlings,
last creatures of their sort.
Survivors of millennia
till humans cut them short.

The endling is a special beast,
though tragic, to be sure.
For once the endling breathes its last,
its species is no more.

Endling:
the last known survivor
of a species or subspecies

The word was coined in the
mid-1990s by Dr. Robert Webster,
a physician from Jasper, Georgia.

Over the past 500 years, thousands of species
of birds, plants and animals have become
extinct. Most endlings die quietly and
anonymously in the wild. But in some rare
cases, humans were there to witness their
final days. These reluctant ambassadors were
given names and have gone on to become
symbols of their tragic species.

Martha
September 1, 1914

Last passenger pigeon
(Ectopistes migratorius)

Once, Martha's cousins filled the skies,
made morning look like night.
Then, one by one, we hunted them
till none were left in sight.

Until the 19th century, the passenger pigeon was the most
plentiful bird in North America, its population numbering in
the billions. Historical accounts describe migrating flocks so massive
they darkened the sky for hours as they passed overhead. Humans'
overhunting quickly and drastically reduced their numbers, and by
1914 only Martha was left. She died at the Cincinnati Zoo, at age 29.

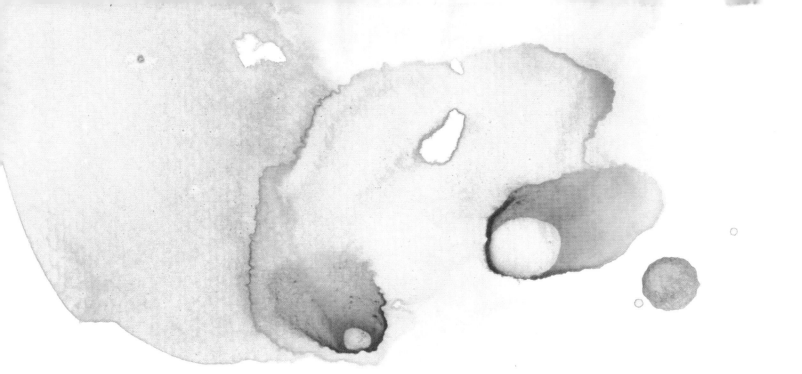

Booming Ben
March 11, 1932

Last heath hen
(Tympanuchus cupido cupido)

Farewell to our dear feathered friend.
We hardly knew you, Ben.
Old photographs are all that's left
of this once-common hen.

Until about 200 years ago, heath hens (a subspecies of the prairie chicken) were a common sight across the plains of the northeastern United States. Sadly, hunting and habitat loss decimated their numbers, and by 1885 the hens had completely disappeared from the mainland. A small population remained on Martha's Vineyard (an island near Cape Cod), but despite determined last-ditch efforts to save the species, the damage had already been done. By 1931 only one heath hen was left. Booming Ben lived as an endling for two years.

Lonesome George
June 24, 2012

Last Pinta Island tortoise
(Chelonoidis abingdonii)

Poor 100-year-old Lonesome George.

His passing we lament.

Did he wonder in those final days

where all the others went?

The giant tortoises of Pinta Island were almost completely wiped out by hunters in the 19th century. The remaining ones died as a result of wild goats being introduced to the habitat—the goats decimated most of the island's vegetation, which had been the tortoises' main source of food. The subspecies was believed to be extinct until, in 1971, a single surviving male was discovered. For the next 40-plus years Lonesome George was known as one of the rarest animals on Earth. He was 100 years old when he died, which is considered quite young for a Pinta Island tortoise.

Incas
February 21, 1918

Last Carolina parakeet
(Conuropsis carolinensis)

Rest in peace, dear little bird.
Your memory will live on
in cautionary tales because
your species is now gone.

Until its extinction, the Carolina parakeet was the only parrot native to the eastern United States. Hunting (it was prized for its colorful feathers), disease and loss of habitat from deforestation all contributed to the species' demise. Incas, the last surviving male, died in captivity at the Cincinnati Zoo after losing his mate, Lady Jane. Incas died in the same cage in which Martha, the last passenger pigeon, had passed away four years earlier.

Benjamin
September 7, 1936

Last Tasmanian tiger
(Thylacinus cynocephalus)

A requiem for Benjamin,
the last one of his kind.
Another one as rare as him
the world will never find.

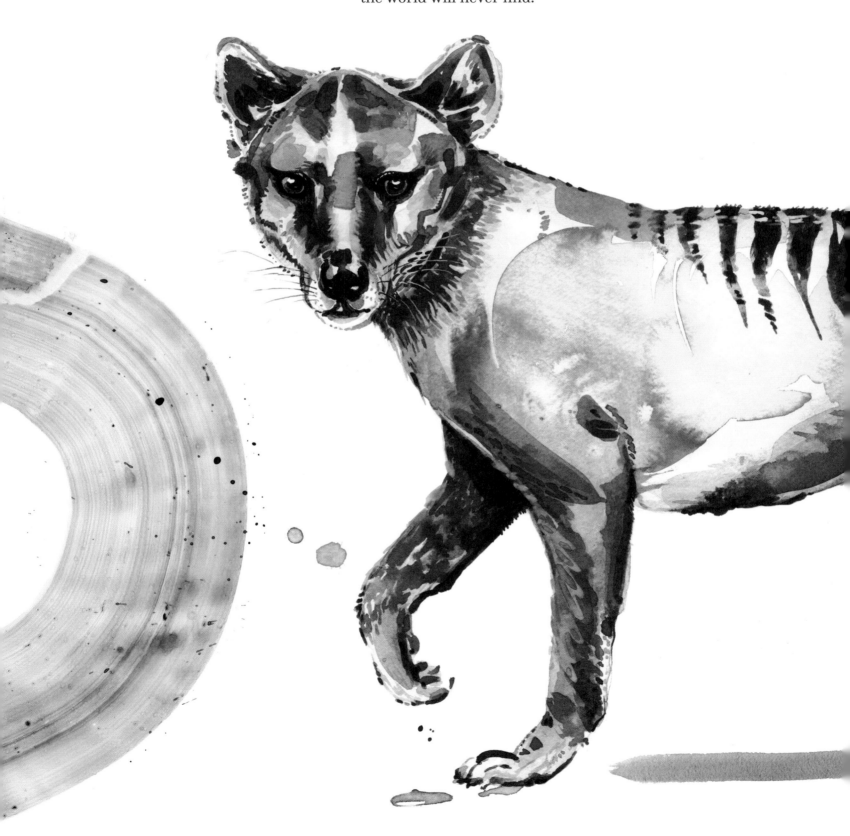

Native to mainland Australia as well as the islands of Tasmania and New Guinea, the Tasmanian tiger (also known as the thylacine) was the world's largest carnivorous marsupial. This unique creature had the face of a coyote, the coloring and stripes of a tiger, and the belly pouch of a kangaroo. A once plentiful species, it was considered a threat to sheep and livestock by colonial settlers. As a result, the Tasmanian government offered a reward to tiger hunters for each one they killed from 1888 to 1909. Due to overhunting and loss of habitat, the world has lost this unique creature. Benjamin, the last of his kind, died of exposure at the Beaumaris Zoo after he was accidentally left out of his enclosure on a cold night.

Celia
January 6, 2000

Last Pyrenean ibex
(Capra pyrenaica pyrenaica)

We will remember Celia,
dear and long departed.
A subspecies extinction that has
left us brokenhearted.

In 1999, scientists discovered that Celia was the only Pyrenean ibex left in the world. Rather than capturing and caging her, they collared her and allowed her to remain in the wild. When Celia was killed in an accident a year later, her cells were preserved for science. The subspecies was able to make a brief comeback in 2003 after scientists successfully cloned Celia. Unfortunately, the newborn lived for just 10 minutes. The Pyrenean ibex now holds the unique distinction of being the only animal in the world to have become extinct twice.

Turgi
January 31, 1996

Last Polynesian tree snail
(Partula turgida)

In ever-loving memory
of Turgi the tree snail.
His disappearance from the world
a sad and tragic tale.

Colonists brought giant African land snails to the Polynesian Islands in the 1800s. The new species destroyed the local snail populations, most of which had been flourishing on the islands for millennia. Turgi the endling passed away in a plastic box at the London Zoo in 1996. Because Polynesian tree snails move so slowly—a rate of less than two feet a year—it took Turgi's keepers a few days to determine that he had died. His grave marker is a tragic tribute to his fallen species. It reads: *1.5 million years BC to January 1996.*

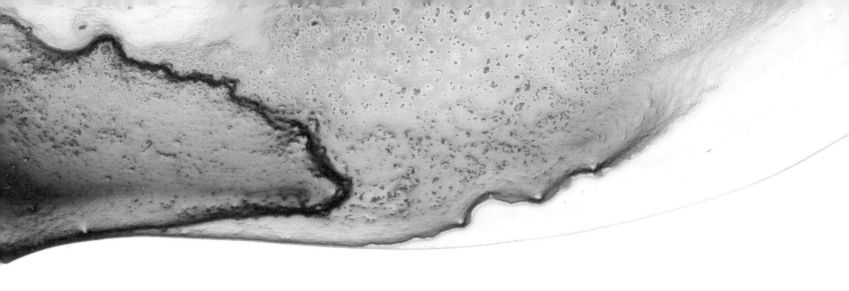

Toughie
September 26, 2016

Last Rabbs' fringe-limbed tree frog
(*Ecnomiohyla rabborum*)

This handsome endling rests in peace.
Oh, fine amphibian!
Sweet Toughie has now hopped away
into oblivion.

Amphibians are the most endangered of all animal groups. Since the 1980s a global amphibian extinction crisis has been underway—it is estimated that a third or more of all amphibian species are currently at risk of disappearing. Amphibian population declines are caused by disease, habitat destruction, pollution and pesticide use, as well as the spread of a deadly fungal disease called *chytridiomycosis*.

Toughie died by himself at the Atlanta Botanical Garden, thousands of miles away from his birthplace in the treetops of Panama. His death has become a tragic symbol of endangered amphibians. His extinction has helped raise awareness about other frog species rapidly vanishing from our planet.

Good reader, I now offer you
a question most complex:
Of these endangered species, which
will have an endling next?

It's possible that the following animals could become extinct by 2050: polar bears, chimpanzees, Sumatran elephants, snow leopards, tigers, lowland gorillas, orangutans, giant pandas, rhinos, sea turtles, rusty-patched bumble bees, monarch butterflies and koala bears.

It's estimated that 50 percent of all species on Earth now could face extinction by 2120.

All life forms on Earth are interconnected. If insects, plants and animals continue to disappear at a rapid rate, life for humans will be irreversibly impacted in ways we can't even begin to imagine.

The biggest threat to our planet's animals, insects and plants comes from habitat loss as a result of human activities such as deforestation, pesticide use, and pollution from industry and agriculture. With ever-shrinking habitats (places to live), thousands of species will eventually die out.

Trying to save our planet's endangered species is a huge job, but there's a lot you can do to make a difference.

"Whatever happens to this single animal, let him always remind us that the fate of all living things on Earth is in human hands."

—Words inscribed outside Lonesome George's enclosure at the Charles Darwin Research Station on Santa Cruz Island

HOW KIDS can make A CHANGE

1. Become a climate activist by spreading awareness. You can do this by sharing books and information with friends and having conversations with your classmates and parents.

2. Avoid single-use plastics like straws or cups.

3. Reduce, reuse or recycle whenever possible.

4. Choose to walk or ride your bike instead of driving.

5. Read books about climate change, extinction and shrinking wildlife habitats.

6. Pass this book along to a friend, and ask them to pass it along after they've read it.

7. Plant a tree or habitat garden at your school or in your backyard.